Little Book of SNAKES

BY: EMILY ATKINSON

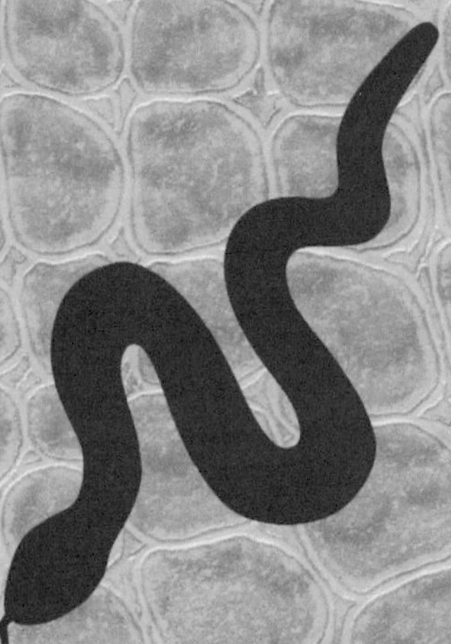

To Jessie
My biggest fan

Little Book of Snakes

Copyright © 2022 by Emily Atkinson

ISBN: 9798366093347
Second Edition

Independently Published

Graphics from Canva and Jackson Smith

My name is Gary and I am a green tree python.

I live in the rainforests of New Guinea.
It is hot and humid where I stay.

When I am young, my body is red or yellow.
I change colors as I grow up.

As an adult, my body is green with white, yellow, and blue spots and stripes. I can get as long as 5 feet.

My favorite foods to eat are birds, small mammals and other reptiles.

I have pits by my mouth and nose that help me sense heat. This allows me to find prey easier, because all animals give off heat.

I am an excellent climber. I spend almost all of my time in the trees. I even sleep wrapped up on a tree limb.
Can you climb trees like me?

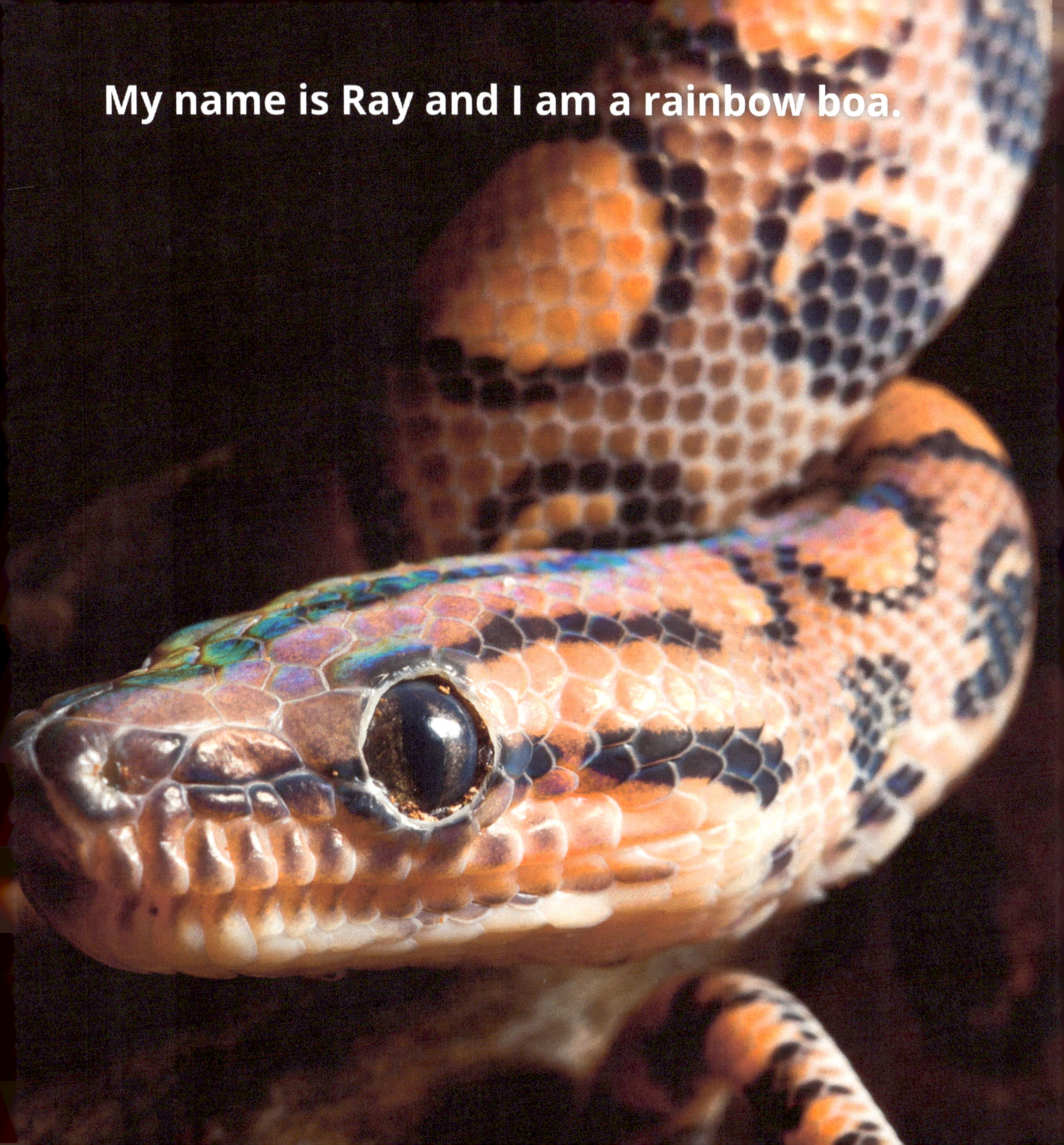
My name is Ray and I am a rainbow boa.

I live in the Amazon River basin in South America. It is warm and very humid where I am.

I am brownish-red with 3 black stripes on my head. I have black rings down my back. I can be up to 6 feet long.

My favorite things to eat are rodents, birds, fish, frogs, and lizards.

I have tiny ridges on my scales that bend the light so it looks like a rainbow. This is why I'm called a rainbow boa.

I have a very thick body,
which can make it hard for me
to move. I move very slowly!
Can you move slow like me?

My name is Edgar. I am an African egg-eating snake

live in the forests of Africa. It is hot and dry here.

I can be light brown or gray with spots and lines along my back. I grow to be up to 2 ½ feet long.

The only food I eat is eggs, which I swallow whole.

I have no teeth, so I don't crack the eggs when I eat them.

After swallowing the egg, I crack it so I can drink the insides. Then I spit out the empty shell.

I have very rough scales that I can rub together and make a hissing sound to scare away predators. Can you rub your hands together to make noise like me?

My name is Cassie and I am a cat-eyed snake.

I live in the forests and grasslands of Mexico and Central America. I always live near ponds or lakes so I can find food easily.

My body is brown, gold, and orange with large blotches along my back. I have a thin body with a big head. I can be up to 2 ½ feet long.

I like to eat frogs, fish, and lizards.

I have large eyes with
upright pupils, just like a
cat. This is why I am
called a cat-eyed snake.

I spend most of my life climbing in the trees at night. Because of my big eyes, I can see very wel in the dark. Can you see in the dark like me?

My name is Wanda. I am a woma python.

I live all over the grasslands and forests of Australia. I live in holes that I dig by using my head like a shovel. It is hot and dry where I stay.

I am yellow and brown with brown bands running down my whole body. I have an orange head with dark scales around my eyes. I can grow up to 8 feet long.

I like to eat birds, eggs, small mammals, and small reptiles.

I am immune to othe
snake's venom. This
means that if a
venomous snake bit
me, I don't get hurt

Because it is so hot where I live, I have a special way of moving. I only let a small part of my belly touch the ground at a time so I don't get burnt, just like tiptoeing.
Can you tiptoe along the ground like me?

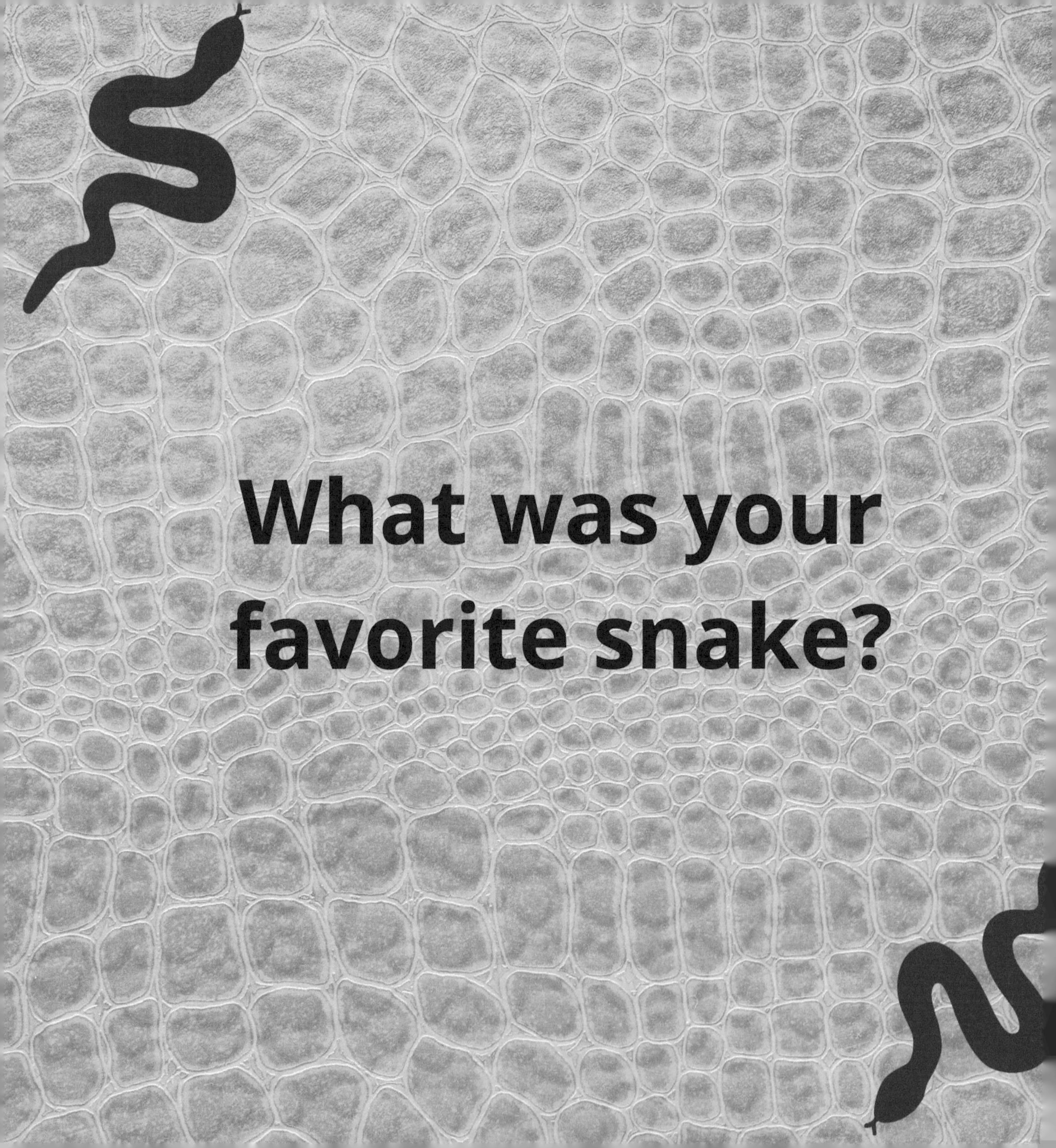

What was your favorite snake?